DR. BARBARA MELAMED

Aging Sucks

UNLESS YOU CROSS THE BRIDGE

ISBN: 979-8-3481-3051-0 (sc)
ISBN: 979-8-3481-3052-7 (e)
ISBN: 979-8-3481-3069-5 (sc)

2024.12.16

This book is printed on acid-free paper.

Because of the dynamic nature of the Internet, any web addresses or links contained in this book may have changed since publication and may no longer be valid. The views expressed in this work are solely those of the author and do not necessarily reflect the views of the publisher, and the publisher hereby disclaims any responsibility for them.

Preface

This booklet will help you and yours **Bridge** the gap from feeling totally in charge to letting go and not covering up. There are many excellent resources for helping us make the step from "I'm okay" to "Watch out… I could use some help." I am going to use a BRIDGE model to help you the reader enhance the crossing from total independence to acceptance of help from another.

Brain health is at the top of the height of the bridge. How do we calibrate where we are on this dimension? First, we need to accept the fact that as we age our brain also changes. More plaques build up which slows the transmission and recall of information we might have had control over at one point. Think of the positiv… recall and memory become more difficult, not because we are slow, but because so much has been encompassed in our life. So, if we turn to the experts and I highly recommend… Chapter 4 is about the Mind, Memory, and Mood which we don't know. Prevention is possible… and we will show you how… but there must be a recognition that dementia may occur if we live too long.

Relationships—Those with more people to care about and be cared for—never stop or we will die sooner.

"I" whether it's okay vs. When I am or putting "I" before the other.

Death is a reality. Deal with it. Get your stuff in order so that you won't feel that you have left a mess for others to clean up.

Grow with the other Generation. Gratitude is a quality of life that incorporates the idea that others play an important role in our lives. Generosity whether it comes from the heart or from expecting something in return does need to focus on who receives your tangible and intangible goods. Social support is one of the predictors of who stays alive longer when dealing with a chronic illness, such as diabetes or rheumatoid arthritis.

Exercise, Eating, and EGO

So, get aboard your cycle, car, caravan… or shoes… and let's *cross over the bridge*. Exercise has been cited as increasing your ability to stay involved with others. Eating with the right, and with whom you share is critical. And EGO like I make one feel in charge of what they do and the sense that they can do what is expected.

An introduction: Why should I read this book?

This book is about becoming aware of what aging does to us and our loved ones. The chapters invite you the reader to put yourself into the areas of life and give you the tools to overcome and become UNSTOPPABLE. OPTIMISM is critically important in staying healthy. Relationships with others both your loved ones, work partners, and medical care providers, and social support you need in times of trouble and joys.

It's important to think about **Death**. On my Deathbed, I would like to be surrounded by people who love me. Well, that means I've got to hear that love between now and then. I've got to say a few wise things to them, which means I have become gratifying between now and then. It is important to give and forgive and enjoy each day as if it was your last. This book allows you to see how behavioral and cognitive strategies will enhance your life. Chapters on optimism and social support and others will engage you in finding your own joys and healthy dependence upon others. Medical views of aging [33] view major diseases of aging as the result of molecular and cellular changes. They are what emerge from epigenetic modifications, stem cell exhaustion, telomere attrition, genomic damage, and sense accumulation, loss of proteostasis, mitochondrial dysfunction, altered cellular communication, and dysregulated nutrient sensing. However, the current book looks

at diet, exercise, and behavioral modification interventions to slow this process.

Jean Carper in *Stop Aging Now!* [22] specified certain antiaging supplements, herbs, and food. For instance, rather than saying exclude all fats, they list olive oil, canola oil, macadamia nut oil, fish oil, flaxseed oil instead of margarine, and cholesterol and animal fats in meat poultry, and dairy products.

Jo Ann Jenkins who is the CEO of the Association of Advancement of Retired Persons has a book called *Disrupt Aging* [27] which captures the sentiment of many aging folks that one should look forward to those years of their life where productivity may be re-imagined as she says to"navigate life's transitions, find meaning and purpose, and get the most of life in a vastly changing world" (p.31). She aptly points out that it's not only how we are going to act… but how society is going to act. The idea put forth is that people need to be valued for who they are not judged for how old they are. Another prominent woman, Jenkins defines our thoughts of legacy as wondering what those we leave behind will remember about us. She points out that the feeling of being wanted and needed is essential to staying longer.

Adrianna Huffington writes in *Thrive* [26], "Success isn't defined just by money or power, but also included well-being, taking care of ourselves, wisdom, the knowledge gained by experience, wonder, delight in the wonders of the universe, and giving, and empathy and compassion for other." She and AARP founder Andrus, fought for health insurance for retirees which would not require a medical exam, be non-cancelable, and be budget capable. A recipient of her award was 76-year-old Elizabeth Dole whose foundation Caring for Military Families provided care not only for the injured military but for their families, who become invaluable caregivers. So to disrupt aging four things are necessary:

1. physical and mental fitness;
2. focus on disease prevention rather than treatment;
3. shift from being dependent patients to empowered users of health care and

4. dependable access to care by having health insurance including coverage for preventive care as well as effective clinical services.

Good health as she says is the great enabler to a long, happy, and meaningful life as it provides the energy and drive to pursue happiness, to carry out our daily roles, to work and volunteer, and to engage in meaningful relationships. So, health is more than the absence of illness, it is what gives us a sense of well-being and vitality to experience meaningful life. Thus, the Affordable Care Act the Google launched Calico, a new healthcare company to help understand aging and age-related diseases. Verizon has an app to alert one to avoid falling. AT&T has invested in telehealth and remote-monitoring devices. Technologies have been identified: information technology, robotics, genetics, user-ship, and service enablers. We continue to need philanthropy such as Habitat for Humanity, which builds homes for people who can't afford to own a home.

So what does *Aging Suck... Unless* provided to the reader? What is this **Bridge** we need to cross and help us make it to the other side where we can enjoy happiness before we must join our loved ones? Take the **Bridge** letters with you every day. For one, it is focused on;

B for Breathing, taking time to enjoy your life.

R is for Relationships. Not only is there hard evidence that you live longer if you have folks you care about… hose who strive to be there for you and you for them.

I is for Independence and your own self-esteem which powers you to continue to feel good about yourself after retirement and in your ability to deal with inevitable stress due to illness or worry.

D is dealing with death. One wants to take care of leaving behind not only a legacy of whom you were but acknowledging that your money is well distributed and that the kind of remembrance you want is mutually shared with the loved ones you will leave behind.

G is for generosity and gratitude. Making sure you let those you love and who love you know that you appreciated them and want to supplement whatever education or job maintenance they have chosen.

And finally, we need to have –

E stands for energy to do what we want to while we are here. And to have our Ego available to do the things we judge necessary.

This book is designed for you so take it to heart, whether you take notes, or start a diary, or photograph things which are important to you. Listening to music, taking a walk observing life in the trees, gardens, and water, and becoming inspired to create your legacy is all important. This book will allow you to formulate that and show you how to communicate it to your loved ones, colleagues, and students. Reading this will give you a sense of completion so you can enjoy the rest of your existence without worrying about unfinished business. So, open it and begin the joy of making things right. And feeling good is the message it brings with ways to accomplish that.

This book is about becoming aware of what aging does to us and our loved ones. The chapters invite you the reader to put yourself into the areas of lifestyles and give you the tools to overcome and become **Unstoppable. Optimism** is critically important in staying healthy. Relationships with others both your loved ones, work partner, and medical care providers provide the social support you need in times of trouble and joy. The Mayo Clinic (2024) has delivered an amazing update on how to stay healthy as we age. Sinclair and LaPlante in the forward to their book *Lifespan* [32] have gifted us with a creative way to stay young. A special issue of *National Geographic* (January, 2023) entitled "Living Longer and Better" [19] describes how science can change the way we age. This amazing issue with actor Chris Hemworth new TV series "Limitless" streaming on Disney plus opens the gate to extending life expectancy. Scientists now understand how our cells age and the four ways they are harmed. The ability now to prevent cell damage allows centurians hope. Research has been underway at the Baltimore Longitudinal Study of Aging (https://www.nia.nih. gov/research/labs/blsa) and followed more than 3200 people assessing cognitive, physical exam on strength with urine samples on over 50 years generating thousands of scientific papers.

It's important to think about **Death**. On my Deathbed, I would like to be surrounded by people who love me. Well, that means I've got to hear that love between now and then I've got to say a few wise things to them, which means I have to become wise between now and then. It is important to give and forgive and enjoy each day as if it was your last, this book allows you to see how behavioral and cognitive strategies will enhance your life. Chapters on optimism and social support and others will

Medical views of aging view major diseases of aging as the result of molecular and cellular changes. They are what emerge from epigenetic modifications, stem cell exhaustion, telomere attrition, genomic damage, and senescence accumulation, loss of proteostasis, mitochondrial dysfunction, altered cellular communication and, dysregulated nutrient sensing. However, the current book looks at diet, exercise, and behavioral modifications can intervene to slow this process. Carper's *Stop Aging Now!* [22] specified certain anti-aging supplements, herbs, and food. For instance, rather than saying exclude all fats, they list olive oil, canola oil, macadamia nut oil, fish oil, flaxseed oil instead of margarine, and cholesterol and animal fats in meat poultry, and dairy products.

The Whole Person Notion is the chosen approach. Why?

The National Center for Complementary and Integrative Health (NCCIH) [40] at the National Institutes of Health (NIH) has embraced the concept of whole-person health to underlie its research effort and drive discovery. Dr. Helene Langevin describes whole person health as "supporting the health and well-being of each person across multiple domains—biological, behavioral, social, and environmental—through research on multicomponent nutritional, psychological, and physical approaches to care." The NCCIH has included the concept of whole-person health in its new strategic plan, which will guide the institute's research endeavors for the next 5 years.

Whole person health is complex, and research in this area is challenging. "Research on whole person health must integrate across physiological systems, explore multicomponent interventions and measure the impact of interventions in multiple organs, systems, and domains," says Dr. Langevin. One potential area of exploration is that of multicomponent approaches such as Traditional Chinese Medicine, Ayurveda, and naturopathy. Other areas, such as nutritional research and stress management research offer unique opportunities for studying whole person health.

Recent research from Bookwala & Gaugler in *Health Psychology* (2020) [2] showed that negative relationship, namely criticism with one's spouse or partner was associated with higher odds for mortality after 5 years. There were no differences for husband or wife. This was true even when age, gender, education self-rated health and medication use were also predictive of mortality.

This was true regardless of family or other social networks the participant had. Women did not produce more deaths regardless of analyses.

This research was done on finding from the National Institutes of Health project on National Social Life, Health and Aging Project [41].

In the area of Aging, Dr. Melamed has already been the recipient of the BioGenesis Health Cluster, Award for her research and studies in aging by the Gerontological Society of America. She is a candidate for the National Center to Reframe Aging National Facilitator Training 2023

Without the assistance of my caregiver as I age from Venezuela, Mariana Gomez, and my daughter Jodi Melamed, author of Represent and Destroy: Rationalizing Violence in the New Racial Capitalism, University of Minnesota Press, 2011 this book would not have been accomplished. My son-in-law Anthony Peressini, Marquette University, was instrumental in making this book an edited miracle for the reader.

My spouse Thomas Wills has been Director of the Prevention Center of the University of Hawaii Cancer Enter, and my son Alex Wills who recently left for college and jobs, and my Service dog, Lincoln and cuddles from Powderpuff my chest purring cat this book would not have been done. My mother Frances and brother Marty were always beside me despite their having left this earth quite a while ago.

Contents

List of Figures

1. Starting the Route over the BRIDGE

Unless what? Gotcha. What will you get out of your booklet? Who should read this booklet and why?

The "UNLESS" in Aging Sucks is inviting you to recognize that you can still be active and be grateful for what you still can do.

This manual is a kind of memoir for yourself. It is private unless you wish to share it with others. YOU WILL CHOOSE A ROAD to go down.

Figure 1.1: The Path

NAME of My ROAD _____________________ (e.g., my road is _________________).
You may choose to be alone on the journey or share your thoughts with another either a family member _____________________ or maybe a TRUSTED friend _____________________ or group _____________________ or even a loved one you lost and want to keep in contact with. (Hey Mom I miss you) _____________________.

So, the above are fillable exercises if you want to write out your journey to share, or retain them for another time in your life. Review every 6 months as you turn 70 years old.

Figure 1.2: Pinocchio and Dumbo.

We all are going through the process of aging. Only "Dumbo" or "Pinocchio "stay the same. Never Lie about your AGE? Our book focuses on family, work, and recreation for those of us over 60 years of age. Another reader would be your primary caretaker, nursing home staff, whether a son/daughter or a partner(spouse) or ex-husband or wife or paid caretaker who needs to understand from your perspective what they need to know about "you" the "aging" person in order to maximize pleasure in your life. This would identify things like (How often you need to be near a bathroom?) which might interfere with your capacity to enjoy reaching your goals. Like going to your granddaughter or grandson's graduation. Date to live for: _______________________. Some background information from YOU the reader which includes medical conditions, mental status, medication, physical limitations (need a cane, breathing app (i.e. Calm) But something to ensure your privacy otherwise you won't have contact with me… and that's okay… use some trusted person close to you in your daily life. Who? _______________________ contact email, phone or text _______________________. Your book starts here and makes AGING a positive rather than negative experience.

So, maybe for a starter let's get rid of the term "Aging" as it sounds like a negative. So, what are some of your ideas for an alternative verb? Perhaps "Being"or "Dreaming" or "Doing." Or Traveling or Swimming?

Your alternative verb: _______________________.

I like the idea of a VERB rather than a NOUN. Although I think "ME" is a good way to think of yourself. Try to be active as you enjoy this manual by completing some of the sentences or blank areas allowing you to review your feelings over time. So number one—**get a pencil and pad** or join me by filling in the following.

Name: Age: How old are you? _______________________, How old do you feel?

Closest Loved One: _______________________

Who do you want bedside when you go if the choice is yours _______________________

Most loving pets _______________________

Name two persons you loved and are gone? (Loved ones already are waiting for you on the other side).

_______________________ and _______________________

So, I introduce myself to you in a few paragraphs with my favorite photographs. Take a look at your photos and pick one to put in the center empty square.

I just turned 80 years young. But some days I wake up and I can't even get out of bed. I ask you the reader to provide me with your favorite photos and a few paragraphs about music you like ___________________________, sports you have played ___________________________, schools you hated ___________________________

    Courses you loved ___________________________.

    Who I am? ___________________________

    Who do I want to be? ___________________________

    My loved ones? ____

    Where do I want to live? ____

    Where do I want to be when I die? ____

So, always wear a life jacket or bring a better swimmer with you. Or better yet sit in your bathtub and eat your cake and enjoy it. We only go around once in this world.

Figure 1.3: The Life Jacket

Even as you age, trips can be arranged in groups where disabilities are considered, and physicians and caregivers are aboard.

Don't be afraid to travel.

Figure 1.4: The traveler!

I travel all around the world: This is Ankar Watt, Cambodia. Come with me later to India, Germany, Russia, Bosnia, Indonesia, New Zealand, Italy, France, Spain, and Denmark.

Also, why do you want to read a book about Aging? Are you having a difficult time accepting changes in your life such as job termination, physical limitations, or illness, which keep you from enjoying things such as sky diving, scuba, sailing, fishing, or having a boat of your own?

I would also like you to use this book as a guide and memoir for yourself to build up your own memories. It might also be a nice gift to leave to your child, one for remembrance of life with you. So, I invite you to use this as a note-taking or photo album, which you can review. Some of us are playing with our obituaries or leaving notes and kisses via the internet. It's okay that way we are still here both for our dream and the memories of those who loved and tolerated you.

Medical

2. How to Find the Right Medical Doctor as we Age?

It is best to have a primary care physician who keeps your records, test results, and any referrals and feedback from other physicians you consult. All in one place is also a way to reduce your family member's ability to be there when you need them and know who can be helpful. It reduces their anxiety to know that person and have the freedom to speak with them at your request.

Osteoporosis Me? At Risk? As we age our bodies often have trouble catching up or too many sidetracks to the doctor, dentist, or gym. First things first. Don't wait until it hurts, check out all systems routinely like you would if you were piloting an airplane.

Table of Systems for routine inspection:

- Oral health
- Mental health
- Cardiovascular health
- Obesity consultation if needed
- Any family inherited dispositions

Also, anger and headaches are symptoms that should be considered part of this routine as they often signal that things are not A-Okay.

Finding the Right Primary Care Physician I DID. Dr. Eugene Lee (see Figure 2.1) "listens," "cares" and is "available 24/7" and he "understands" "helps reduce worries" and never laughs at my questions or me.

Definition: Osteoporosis It is a bone disease that affects approximately 10 million people in the U.S. Women are more likely to suffer. When the bones become brittle and weak... even a minor fall or bending over or coughing could cause a broken bone.

Most Affected: 80% of women are likely to fall victim and white and Asian women of older ages are most likely to suffer especially in hip and spine injuries. Post-menopausal women at risk.

Prevention: UNDER SUPERVISION:

- Weight-bearing exercise especially aerobic activities
- Flexibility exercises
- Strength training-use your muscles
- Stability and balance

Habit changes: Cut out smoking. Reduce alcohol consumption. Don't use screen time including telephones as you lay down to bed. There are watches you can wear which allow you to monitor screen time and provide you with reminders for heart-healthy activities and check on your oxygen consumption as you breathe.

Figure 2.1: Dr. Lee and me!

Medication: Vitamin D 50,000 units, once/week, then switch to 600 Units I am not a Medical Doctor and you need to check frequently when several medicines are prescribed by different doctors that they are all aware of dosage and changes. The pharmacist has an app to make sure you are aware of any of these that have been prescribed.

Aging and Dental Health: Older adults are at increased risk for root caries because of both increased gingival recession that exposes root surfaces and increased use of medications that produce xerostomia; approximately 50% of persons aged older than 75 years of age have root caries affecting at least one tooth. Ten percent of patients 75 to 84 years of age are affected by secondary coronal caries; this is likely related to the prevalence of restorations in the older population. Adoption of good oral hygiene, which includes use of rotating/oscillating toothbrushes, and the use of topical fluoride (i.e., daily mouth rinses, high fluoride toothpaste and regular fluoride varnish application), as well as attention to dietary intake have been recommended in the literature, [18].

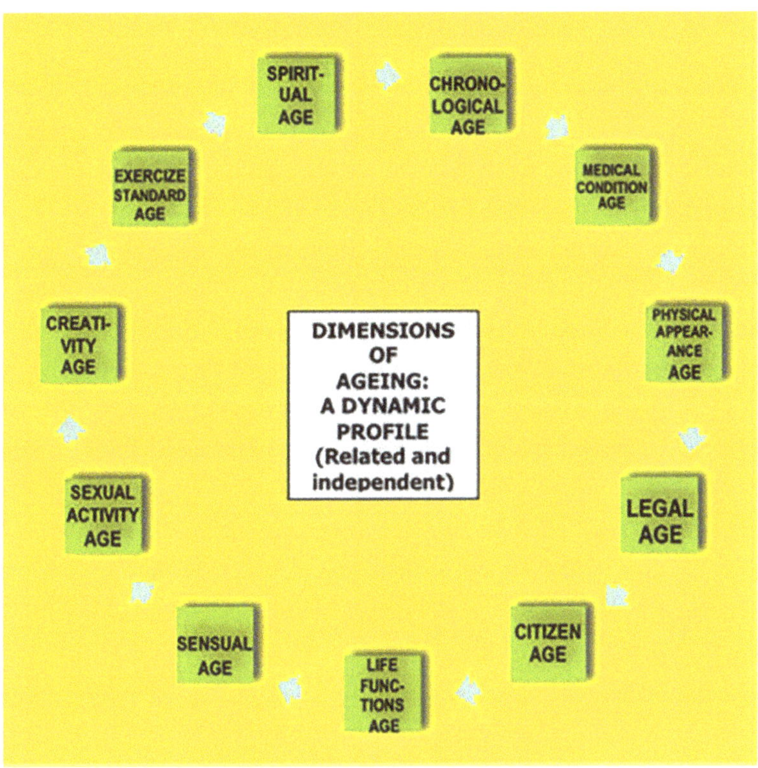

Figure 3.1: Dimensions of Aging.

3.1   What Stage was I?

Dr. Anthony Marsella [30] a well-known expert on culture and health sites acknowledgment the importance of Chinese history and notably how different cultures view changes in life's path.

- Medical-Condition Age: Refers to your medical or health condition. I had a lot OF sicknesses and more medication than my chart could handle. What illnesses have you conquered and what do you still have to deal with?
- Physical-Appearance Age: Refers to whether or not your physical appearance – especially facial and body features and attractiveness – is commensurate with your

chronological age. This, of course, is based on the assumption everyone ages in accord with their age, independent of life experiences, genes, diet, and access to vitamins and blenders. Plastic surgery and various health-promotion techniques have made it possible to appear one age while chronologically being another age. This, of course, is based on the assumption everyone ages in accord with their age, independent of Physical-Appearance Age: Refers to whether or not your physical appearance – especially facial and body features and attractiveness – is commensurate with your chronological age.

What stage are you at? ____

And why? ____

And What Stage is your closest partner, child, love-one at? ________________

Professor Hwang [35] a Taiwanese-born psychologist, trained in graduate school at the University of Hawaii in social and cultural psychology, began to explore the thoughts and writings of the ancient venerated Chinese sage, Confucius (551 BCE–479 BCE), with special attention to the role of Confucian ideas in shaping Chinese psychology across the ages. Professor Hwang's studies revealed the profound impact of Confucian thought for understanding Chinese psychology and behavior, even within the brief period of Communist and Maoist political domination. In a series of publications that now have important historical implications for psychology, Professor Hwang documented the relationship between Chinese psychology and behavior and Confucian thought, especially the critical role of relations. Professor Hwang noted that Confucian thought places heavy emphasis on morality, context, and the nature of interpersonal relationships

Mind and Body

4. Mind, Memory and Mood

4.1 Sleep

Sleep is vital, whether it's a nap on the couch or 6-7 hours on a bed. Make sure your primary care physician is aware of any problems that can be helped.

Figure 4.1: Sleeping Beauty.

Sleep Apnea and Other Sleep Problems

Definition 4.1 — Sleep Apnea. A common and serious disorder in which breathing repeatedly stops for 10 seconds or more during sleep. The disorder results in less oxygen in the blood and can briefly awaken sleepers throughout the night (adapted from WebMD). There are two main types:

- **Definition 4.2 — Obstructive Sleep Apnea (OSA).** It happens when there's a problem with the mechanics of your breathing.
- **Definition 4.3 — Central sleep apnea (CSA).** is when you regularly stop breathing while you sleep because your brain doesn't tell your muscles to take in air. It's different from obstructive sleep apnea, in which something physically blocks your breathing.

But you can have both kinds together, called mixed sleep apnea. Central sleep apnea usually happens because of a serious illness, especially one that affects your lower brainstem, which controls breathing.

The most affected are people over age 65: it's estimated that at least 10% have the condition. Aging affects the brain's ability to keep upper airway throat muscles stiff during sleep, increasing the chance that the airway will narrow or collapse.

Obstructive sleep apnea is up to four times as common in men as in women, but women are more likely to have sleep apnea during pregnancy and after menopause. In older adults, the gender gap narrows after women reach menopause.

Central Sleep Apnea is likely to cause:
- Being very tired during the day.
- Waking up often during the night.
- Having headaches in the early morning.
- Trouble concentrating.
- Memory and mood problems.
- Not being able to exercise as much as usual.

If left untreated it can lead to heart disease, stroke, and death.

Prevention: Obesity and smoking are problematic. Reduce the use of sleep medication and alcohol consumption. Exercise is also important in maintaining weight loss and healthy lungs. Too many things are out there what should I do? Join a group? Set a time? Do it virtually?

Medication: Continuous Positive Airway Pressure (CPAP) machines are available which help the breathing stay rhythmic preventing sleep apnea. Melatonin and other sleep medicines when used occasionally are helpful.

Food: Cut out high-calorie food. Sugar substitutes should be considered. Plant-based diets are often better as we age than meat-focused.

Habit changes: Cut out smoking. Reduce alcohol consumption. Don't use screen time including telephones as you lay down to bed. There are watches you can wear which allow you to monitor screen time and provide you with reminders for heart-healthy activities and check on your oxygen consumption as you breathe.

What helped you? ____

Who helped you? ____

How long did it take to recover? _______________________________________

Did you want to give up? _____________________________________

Did you try again? ____

5. Defeating Memory Loss

Some researchers argue that only the "health span"—the period of life free of illness—is worth extending. Of course, a healthy lifestyle can add years to most of people's lives and actually improve cellular aging. Some of the biggest payoffs come from quitting or never smoking, logging more than 5½ hours of physical activity per week, and keeping a normal weight.

Drugs (prescribed by your trusted doctor) may be able to do that as well by interrupting common markers of aging, including telomere length, inflammation, oxidative stress, and slower cell metabolism. "That's because you haven't stopped aging," says Jay Olshansky, PhD, a professor of epidemiology and biostatistics at the University of Illinois at Chicago School of Public Health (quoted in [37]). "Yet even if we discover cures to these and all other chronic conditions, it won't change our ultimate prognosis: death." [37] And I will devote an entire chapter to planning it. The Queen of England had quite a celebration—after 90 years of full-time work—so can you. But what if we could? What if we are trying to extend longevity in the wrong way? Instead of focusing on diseases, should we take aim at aging itself? What does this mean? How can we prolong the things which make us happy? We all forget things from time to time. Distraction leads to a lack of concentration as does depression. Now as you approach your 50s it seems to take a greater toll on your health. If you don't remember to take your medicine on time you may forget appointments. Now we must look at the reasons so we can help you minimize the problems. The brain does change over time, and it is important to understand how memories are stored and what may affect their ability to be retrieved and used. It is important to understand that emotional and physical states can also influence memory. It is important to let your physician know you are having problems as a neuropsychologist or neurologist may be able to allay your anxiety by administering a few tests.

For example:

- When was the last time you washed your clothing? ________________________________
- Did you forget the password for your computer? ______________________________

For a better test see https://www.memorylosstest.com/working-memory-training-online/.

It is critically important to be aware of the 10 signs of dementia leading to Alzheimer's disease [38]:

1. Difficulty with everyday tasks. I.e. Keeping track of monthly bills. Difficulty concentrating or taking longer to finish tasks.
2. Repetition. Asking questions over and over or telling the same story.

3. Communication problems. Difficulty joining a conversation and struggles to think of works or names of objects.
4. Getting lost. Difficulty with visual and spatial abilities. I.e. getting lost while driving.
5. Personality changes. Acting unusually anxious, confused, fearful, or suspicious] put easily upset, sometimes depressed.
6. Confustion about time and place. Can't remember how they got someplace, forgetting what the day of the week was.
7. Misplacing things. Putting things in unusual places and having difficulty retracing their steps to find misplaced objects.
8. Troubling Behavior. Poor judgment in handling money or neglects grooming and cleanliness.
9. Loss of interest, or apathy. Loss of interest in family, friends, work, and social events.
10. Forgetting old memories. Memory loss becoming more persistent.

Different types of dementia as well as mixed types such as Alzheimer's and vascular dementia.
1. Affect brain chemistry leading to problems with behavior, and mood. Movement and thinking.
2. Frontotemporal disorders. Degenerative damage of the brain's frontal and temporal lobes is mostly in people aged 65 and younger. Symptoms include apathy, difficulty in communicating, walking or working emotional changes, and impulsive or inappropriate behavior.

So, what do you need to do to preserve function?
1. Engage in cognitively stimulating activities, reading, writing, keeping a memoir, or game playing with a friend i.e. checkers, cards.
2. Make sure the medications you are taking aren't stealing your memory. Discuss the side effects with your physician. Antidepressants, sleeping pills, anti-anxiety drugs, pain medication, and antihistamines do affect memory. Smoking and Alcohol don't help. It helps to include your partner if these discussions can be brought home.
3. Practice mindfulness meditation to focus on the breath (Free app on internet called CALM). You can find a place to focus on, whether watching the fish in your fish tank, or looking at the birds in the trees....ocus your attention for 10 to 15 minutes twice a day. Groups can be helpful as they get you out of your home and it doesn't hurt to share with buddies.
4. If you are having significant problems with learning new skills than you used to or if you can't even comfortably keep up with your accounting then it is time to seek advice. Having a trusted family member or even a home care aide can give you time for the things you love rather than those that are necessary but drain your energy and make you nervous.

Dementia is a progressive disease and there is evidence it can be slowed down. An excellent new book by Dr. Bredesen, *The End of Alzheimer's* program [21] describes how to enhance cognition and reverse the decline. Alzheimer's disease is now one of the leading causes of morbidity and mortality in the world. There are specific recommendations based on research studies that involve for instance a KetoFLEX 12/3 program requiring fasting, exercising, and shifting primarily from burning glucose to burning fat to achieve a mild level of ketosis. Ketones, produced by the liver can fuel the brain very effectively, but the brain still needs glucose. This is a lifestyle program, where FLEX refers to restoring the body's innate ability to metabolize either fat or sugar while maintaining insulin sensitivity. The 12/3 refers to 12 hours' time between the last meal in the evening and the first of the day. The 3 refers to at least three hours between dinner and bedtime. Although Alzheimer's disease is thought to worsen over time, prevention of progression is possible. Look at the early life factors which modify risk:

1. Early life <18 yrs. of age….et a good education.
2. Mid-life 45-65 yrs. Take care of hearing loss, hypertension, and obesity.
3. Late Life Factors older than 65 Smoking, depression, diabetes, physical inactivity, and social isolation.

With this knowledge and the excellent programs described in detail in Bredesen's excellent book, we have control over the activation and destruction of Alzheimer's disease.

Hara Marano in *Psychology Today* [15] discusses how a Mediterranean diet pumped up with plant polyphenols can delay brain aging. While age is the strongest risk factor for neurodegenerative conditions not everyone succumbs. Cognitive decline including dementia and Alzheimer's disease, may be in part a metabolic disorder, a disturbance in fuel operations by the brain. The raging metabolic furnace of the brain spews our highly unstable free radicals of oxygen that damage the machinery of cells and their protective membranes. An antioxidant such as those with the Mediterranean diet is protective. The plant-based foods ensure a steady supply of agents to disarm free radicals. Thus, fruits and vegetables are good antioxidants to limit damage, polyphenols are produced.

5.1 Cognitive Rehabilitation

The are rehabilitative remedies to two important memory diseases:
1. Alzheimer's disease- characterized by amyloid plaques and tangled fibers in the brain and by loss of connections between nerve cells. Damage initially in the hippocampus. But spreads to other areas.
2. Vascular dementia. The second most common type of dementia results from damage to the vessels that supply blood to the brain. Effect focus, organization, problem-solving, and speed of thinking.

Because with Lewy body dementia, the cause is abnormal protein in the brain. For these Lewy bodies, there are many cognitive and behavioral therapies that can be attempted in slowing down progression and assisting us in having a life worth living. The Alzheimer's Association recommends improving communication sometimes having a caregiver will help have **meaningful activities in an established routine** that can create a safe environment for growth and recovery.

What do you like to do?

Watch TV ____

Sporting Events (participant/viewer) ____

Cooking ____

Cleaning/Organizing ____

Watching grandkids ____

Walking the dog ____

Shopping ________________________________

Television viewing in late life is negatively related to health. In a recent study [9], over 37% of aging individuals report watching television alone or with a friend or relative. When watched alone they reported greater loneliness and more sedentary movements.

Society and Relationships

6. What is Ageism?

How do I know I am getting old? Who has the right to decide? What are the consequences of Age discrimination on the individual and on society? What is the relationship between one's concept of self-aging and recovery from disability? Are there different cultural stereotypes which lead to longer life?

Why do we care?

This is a public health crisis and we need to understand how to help those who are in need of elder care. It is also clear that there is discrimination in many areas that face us as we age?

This book is given to you as a guide to help you understand your own course toward end of life. The American Society on Aging just declared Ageism Awareness Day, October, 2023. They have defined ageism as the stereotypes (how we think), prejudice (how we feel) and discrimination (how we act) toward others or oneself. They describe forms of ageism:

Internalized ageism: How we feel about ourselves as aging people. And how we older adults marginalize and discriminate against other older people.

Cultural ageism: The everyday, invisible profoundly ingrained and normalized negative messages about aging and old people embedded in movies, TV songs, jokes.

Implicit ageism: The unconscious bias that includes attitudes, feelings and behaviors toward people of other age groups that operates without conscious awareness or intention.

Benevolent ageism: patronizing, paternalistic beliefs or behaviors that older people need to be protected and taken care of by younger people, because they are no longer able to make decisions for themselves.

We are all different. Some of us keep jobs until the end of our active life whereas others are either forced into retirement or forced into bed by various illnesses. It also affects those around us how we age. Do we have control or is it taken away from us? I have just turned 80 years and will take this voyage with you and yours.

Ageism is a fact. We try with creams and tight-fitting jeans, but believe me when you are almost 80 it shows.

Ageism is considered to include three dimensions: stereotypes (cognitive component—e.g., I think older adults are a burden to society); prejudice (emotional component—e.g., I do not enjoy conversations with older adults); and discrimination (behavioral component—e.g., I try not to interact with older adults [11]). It can be directed towards others (e.g., I enjoy telling jokes about older adults) or towards oneself (e.g., I am concerned about my own aging [36]), it can be positive (e.g., the stereotype that older adults are wise) or negative (e.g., the stereotype that older adults are slow), and it can be explicit (conscious) or implicit (unconscious) [13]. There is no good scale of AGEISM so let's begin with us... yes, you and me.

When I say I am getting old? What do I want my family, friends and fellow workers to take from that?

_________________________ Leave me alone get someone else to do the work?

_________________________ I need help with X, but I am embarrassed to ask.

_________________________ Don't exclude me because I am slow to join. Discussion?

_________________________ Whatever? You're feeling today.

Aging and Disability Older persons with positive age stereotypes were 44% more likely to fully recover from severe disability than those with negative age stereotypes. The study was limited by recruitment from one community; however, its demography is similar to the US population, except for an underrepresentation of black participants. Further research is needed to determine whether interventions to promote positive age stereotypes could extend independent living in later life [14].

Explanatory factor: age stereotypes (defined as beliefs about old people as a category). Positive age stereotypes may promote recovery from disability through several pathways: limiting cardiovascular response to stress, improving physical balance enhancing self-efficacy, and increasing engagement in healthy behaviors. We hypothesized that older persons with positive age stereotypes would be more likely to recover from a disability than those with negative age stereotypes. Recovery was based on 4 essential activities of daily living (ADLs; bathing, dressing, transferring, and walking) that are strongly associated with the use of health care services and longevity.

There was a recent news article explaining that older individuals could not refinance their mortgages or get other loans strictly due to their age. Even if they had the financial resources, companies discriminated against them strictly because of age [42].

We all need to plan so that the moment we are gone our loved ones can breathe a sigh of relief and joy at how our lives have left them with feelings of love and caring so that death rather than the end is the beginning of what we meant to them at our most lively days.

I have already written my obituary open to revision as I continue to be here. But it made me thank those whose love added to my life's pleasures. I think it is important to leave a memoir or a photograph album that can be shared among those who care. Not an obligation but a choice.

George Vaillant writes in *Aging Well* [34] that how life is experienced is more important than medicine, exercise, and nutrition. He inspires us to choose a lifestyle that means something meaningful to us and is shared with someone else before our time is passed. He maintains that winter gardens we need to think of were not only an end but a beginning. He cites Sophocles who sets his tragedy in a garden... in a sacred grove of vines and olive trees in which nightingales sang. And thus Oedipus, a wretched, exiled beggar without sight, turns to acknowledge to his daughter the fate of a man near death, the fate of a garden prepared for winter. He acknowledged to his daughter, "Now that I have and hold what is most dear to me, I am not afraid to die."

So, whether we are in a care facility, hospital or hopefully in our own bed being surrounded by even one loved one will allow a calmer feeling of being. We need to realize that through our loved ones our presence is still felt. It is good to leave remembrances… even an old smelly shirt might be wanted for a while as we are gone forever but we are still felt.

Jane Fonda is 85 years young and calls this chapter of her life the happiest I've ever been. She's weathered controversy for her 70's antiwar activism and started fitness videos. Despite dealing with Hodgkin's Lymphoma and she is still making movies. She does recognize that death will occur. She says, "On my deathbed, I would like to be surrounded by people who love me." She states in an interview in People magazine [39] that she spent a lot of time like a canoe with no paddle being carried in the current. As I got older, "I learned I'm going to put an oar in the water and steer." She also said: "One great thing about aging is all the memories. Be Intentional about how you live your life." So, what does it mean to be "intentional?"

What does retirement mean to you? To me, a bit of re-tire means being tired again. But if done with a plan it may mean a new beginning. Even, as Ralph Waldo Emerson dying of leukemia and racked with pain said, "….t is hard to be happy all the time—but joy, wonder, curiosity, and humor remain." Emerson became the most widely known man of letters in America, establishing himself as a prolific poet, essayist, popular lecturer, and an advocate of social reforms who was nevertheless suspicious of reform and reformers.

So, think about what you have put off doing… maybe a trip to visit an old Auntie or a river ride on one of those Viking tours. You can decide and no one else can fault you for it. Think about what you found enjoyable and be grateful. Successful aging means not dying last but living well. Eric Erikson suggested that one of the life tasks of Integrity is for the old to show the young how not to fear death [25]. Vaillant provides a scale of Graceful Aging and the key evaluative criteria are worth sharing here in brief:

1. Maintains social utility, open to new ideas, cares about others (within the limits of physical health).
2. Eriksonian Integrity, accepts the past and can take sustenance from past accomplishments.
3. Maintains other Eriksonian skills: Basic Trust (hope in life), sensible Autonomy, and Initiative. (In old age Industry, Generativity, and Intimacy are not always possible).
4. Enjoys life, retains sense of humor, capacity for joy and play. (Since "old age is not for sissies," happiness may be possible).
5. Cheerful acceptance of "indignities of old age," graceful about dependency issues, takes care of self, and when ill becomes a patient that a doctor would want to care for.
6. Cultivates relationships with surviving old friends and is successful in making new ones.

Activity Try to be active as you enjoy this book, so please complete some of the sentences or blank areas below, which will allow you to review your feelings over time.

Figure 6.1: Empty Frame for Favorite Photo.

I ask you, the reader, to provide above your favorite photo. And a few paragraphs about:

Who I am? ____

What (else) do I want to be? ____

My loved ones are: ____

Where I want to live. ____

7. Importance of Relationships and Disease

The treatment of cardiovascular risk factors has benefited middle-aged and older people, for example, and new more effective treatment of acute cardiovascular events has substantially reduced their morbidity and mortality.

Emerging chemotherapy and immunotherapeutic treatments are giving new hope to patients with cancer, the second most frequent cause of death in the adult population.

Despite landmark successes in the prevention and treatment of specific diseases, the care of older patients with complex multi-morbidity, defined as two or more chronic medical conditions in the same individual, which represents the major victim patients in the health-care system, has changed little and remains substantially unsatisfactory.

In a special issue of the Journal of Gerontology, a gene called the Forkhead FOXO3 was found to predict resilience in lifespan, health span, and death span [7]. In a study of Japanese-American men conducted in Honolulu at the Kaukini Honolulu Heart Program men who were 45-65 were evaluated for cognitive function, health, and genetic risk factors, they were then assessed 20 years later. *In looking at maintainers vs. decliners they were found to have 1) better education, a diagnosis of CHD, and a higher prevalence of the longevity-associated APOE allele and Forkheadbox FOXO3 G-allele of the singular nucleotide polymorphisms (SNP).* **Decliners were more likely to be older, and have had a prior stroke, Parkinson's disease, dementia, greater baseline depressive symptoms, and possess the APOEe2 Allele.**

The question is it possible to alter the function of FOXO3 by activation? One of these ways it acts is to reduce the negative effects of air pollution. So this is an important factor in the Chinese population. It was found that alteration of the FOXO3 relative to a non-protective allele led to greater life span in older people, females, and those living in low-level pollution exposure [12].

And what about CANCER as we age? The INTEGRATE study represents an important contribution to better inform the management of older adults with cancer, while documenting the quality of life and health-care utilization benefits associated with an oncogeriatric care approach and, thus, laying the foundation for implementation research in geriatric oncology. Wee Kheng Soo and colleagues have shown that the provision of comprehensive geriatric assessment (CGA) also improves the quality of life and healthcare delivery for this specific population [17]. Specifically, participants assigned to integrated oncogeriatric care reported better quality of life, measured by the Elderly Functional Index, over 24 weeks compared with those in the usual care group (overall main effect of group: $t = 2.1$, $df = 213$, $p = 0.039$; effectsize = 0.38). The integrated oncogeriatric care group also had significantly fewer unplanned hospital admissions at 24 weeks (multivariable-adjusted incidence rate ratio 0.60 [95% CI 0.42—0.87]; p = .0066) than the usual care group. These findings lend further support to international consensus recommending the routine inclusion of geriatric assessment-driven interventions in the care of this specific population.

Given the possible feedback loop between morbidity and the rate of aging, addressing incipient disease in the preclinical period might be a powerful strategy to slow down the rate of aging and prevent or delay its deleterious consequences. Over time, treatment approaches that result in poor outcomes could be weeded out and new therapeutic approaches that become available can be tested in real-world situations. Those who care for older adults are fully aware that behavioral, social, and environmental factors can strongly affect the outcomes of older patients with complex multi-morbidity and disability.

Relationships are really important. Even if your mom has lost a partner, her need to cuddle up with those who are still around is profound.

MAKING THERAPY POSSIBLE via Facebook or Zoom A Virtual Activity Program was attempted by James Doorley (et al., 2022) using the Zoom presentation of Active Brains-Fitbit, a group mind-body activity program adapted to show the improvements in physical, cognitive, and emotional functioning in older adults with Chronic Pain and Cognitive Decline [8]. There were significant differences in the positive direction as compared to an in-person attention control group. The participants improved in multimodal physical function, emotional function (anxiety), cognitive function, pain intensity, and coping.

A helpful mental status and decline in aging questionnaire can be found at https://geriatrics.stanford.edu/wp-content/uploads/downloads/culturemed/overview/assessment/downloads/spmsq_tool.pdf

8. Optimism Versus Pessimism

Losing loved ones is inevitable. How I live is under loss is important. What losses affect you? Are you ready to take the LOT (Learned Optimism Test)?

Do it online if you feel up to being honest with yourself: https://www.seemypersonality.com

I did and this is what I learned about myself.

Optimism/Pessimism results :

Optimism: You sometimes believe that the future holds positive opportunities with successful outcomes. Holding on to this will help you to cope with stressful situations and help with your motivation and persistence.

Pessimism: You often view the world as a place of bad experiences and events, you are unlikely to invest much trust or faith in the belief that things will turn out ok.

We need to continue family relationships particularly when a loved one is no longer with us. Whether a mother or dad… a brother or sister… or another… we need first to accept the inevitable and celebrate their life. Who are they to you? That's what really matters now that they are gone. Do you feel you were present with them at the end? Yes, having a funeral is part of the process. Spread what they stood for whether you agreed with all they felt was important. Or not… You are there to bury or spread their remains… you are part of saying goodbye. You came. if possible and if not… you had that phone call with their other… whether mate or son or daughter you felt the loved ones' pain. You need to now be optimistic rather than pessimistic. Optimism is thinking and acting as if their life meant something. Start with you.

How did being around them make you feel better? Did it give you the strength to carry on? Talk now about 3 elders who are still here (specify pet name, age/sex, and purpose) and what they inspire in you.

So, say goodbye to your loved one, mom/dad/life's partner/sister/brother or cousins and aunts. NOW CHOOSE one… someone recent or someone who still inspires you even if they are physically gone and fill out the following:

What was their name? ________________________________

What did you call them? ________________________________

Did you know they would be leaving the earth as we know it? ________________________________

How much time did you have to prepare? ________________________________

Who helped? ________________________________

Who got in your way? ________________________________

How can you keep them in your life? ________________________________

What do you want to be able to share with them when you meet up again? ________________________________

What would they tell you to do now to live more fully? ________________________________

It is unfortunately true that access to end-of-life care and services is unequal on the basis of race, gender, class, and other social identities in America [6]. According to Lisa Bowleg [3], we need to think of death not as good or bad, but as a continuum that needs to be approached with cultural competence and individual differences. As a society, we need to fund low-income home health and hospice options for those who cannot afford substantial care. By increasing patient education on end-of-life care we must pay attention to the fact that by 2050 approximately 40% of Americans ages 65 and older will be Black American, Hispanic, Asian, American Indian, or Alaska Native, which will lead to unequal access to services if we don't do anything. Rather than hide "dying" we need to normalize what it would take for hospice personnel to help their patients achieve the deaths they want. We live in a death-phobic culture of America and we need to address the inequalities.

Food : We know there are different opinions and some depend upon your health condition, but in general… make sure your fridge has something you like… each in for it at least twice or four times a week… whether it's ice cream or sugar soda pop or something less risky like a carrot or an apple. Go for it. Your intake depends on your output as well. Sometimes skipping a meal is okay, dinner is better than breakfast. It's also good to have a "stop" by having the high-calorie treats frozen or wrapped in "pink" paper as a reminder of better things to choose.

Habit Changes : It is most important to remain physically active. Seek at least 30 minutes of moderate to vigorous physical activity most days of the week. These can include things you do anyway like a brisk walk, gardening, or walking the dog. Volunteering may be a positive for both physical, cognitive and mental health. Try to live in a neighborhood where you don't need to drive a car to buy groceries, or visit with family or friends. A sense of belonging is good for both mental and physical health. As we age one thing doesn't change… we need sleep to re-energize our bodies and it is a hard thing to come by. The need to do the same thing every night is important. Get in a habit which involves having your favorite lights on, television off, telephone ready for any emergency. If sleep doesn't come easy… when get up and do something you dislike. Washing the dishes, sorting the laundry, checking on the mail which needs to go out before Tuesday. In other words….ake going to sleep more enjoyable than checking up on the things undone and need to be done tomorrow. Perhaps the world will explode… climate change will take over… you may never see the sun come up… come on go to bed as your mom used to say. For some of us, saying a prayer or putting the dog or cat to sleep first embodies us to close down ourselves.

One of my own studies [4] demonstrated the importance of psychological factors and coping strategies in the social and psychological functioning of individuals with RA, a chronic and progressive disabling rheumatic illness. How effective, a coping strategy should be taught that is directly relevant to a specific disease-related problem at a given time.

In consideration of the three psychological determinants of optimism, perceived social support, and arthritis helplessness, only optimism was found to predict increases in psychosocial adjustment over time regardless of the individual's level of disability. Since optimism also related to positive psychosocial adjustment at each time point, we may explore that successful episodes of coping build up an optimistic construct, in which the patient develops a view of oneself as being able to cope both across time and across stressors.

8.1 Genetic and Psychological Predictors of Aging

Healthy aging is an equity issue, and a social justice issue. The World Health Organization has proposed a definition of "healthy aging" that takes the specific situation of older people into account, namely as "the process of developing and maintaining the functional ability that enables well-being in older age," where functional ability denotes the "attributes that enable people to be and to do what they have reason to value."

The factors influencing health with age is hugely unequal globally, within and across communities, reinforcing social and structural inequalities. This disparity leads to lower life expectancy with poorer quality of life and health for those living with disadvantage. Examples abound, and worse outcomes due to poor air quality or high alcohol intake are concentrated in lower socioeconomic groups.

Education and relative wealth, as markers of inequity, have independent effects on healthy aging trajectories, and cumulative disadvantage due to low education and poverty impacting health persistently across life stages. Sustainable Developmental Goals 9 (SDG) were devised with sustainable developmental goals. The SDGs are designed to achieve a better and more sustainable future for all.

Explicit links between healthy aging and SDGs have focused on SDG3: "to ensure healthy lives and promote wellbeing for all at all ages." If aging is to be sustainable, tangible efforts must be made well beyond this with action across the Goals. Figure 8.1 provides a map of manifest, urgent, opportunities for effective cross life course interdisciplinary approaches for sustainable and equitable healthy aging.

It is mportant to work with those who lived before us. They have a lifetime of experiences to draw upon. They are strongly motivated as they don't have time to fool around.

Ageism : Includes the idea of elder abuse. We have problems coding precursors as this is often hidden in the family. Even the physicians are reluctant to use the ICD code on elder abuse as they don't want to alienate the family or prematurely make a report to authorities. There is a disparity leads to lower life expectancy with poorer quality of life and health for those living with disadvantage. Examples abound, and worse outcomes due to poor air quality or high alcohol intake are concentrated in lower socioeconomic groups. The Table accessible through the website definitely looks at the antecedent behaviors which lead to longer life. Digital ageism is in need of development for AI researchers in collaboration with those aging and already showing some cognitive declines. Recent work by David Chu [24] discusses what it would take for Artificial Intelligence to become accessible for older adults. It is important to fight paternalistic stereotypes offered with harmful "compassionate" ageism, since ". stereotypes concerning older persons that have permeated public rhetoric. Internalized negative stereotypes can cause older adults to experience a decline in cognitive (i.e., memory) and psychological performances" [10].

Education and relative wealth, as markers of inequity, have independent effects on healthy aging trajectories, and cumulative disadvantage due to low education and poverty impacting health persistently across life stages.

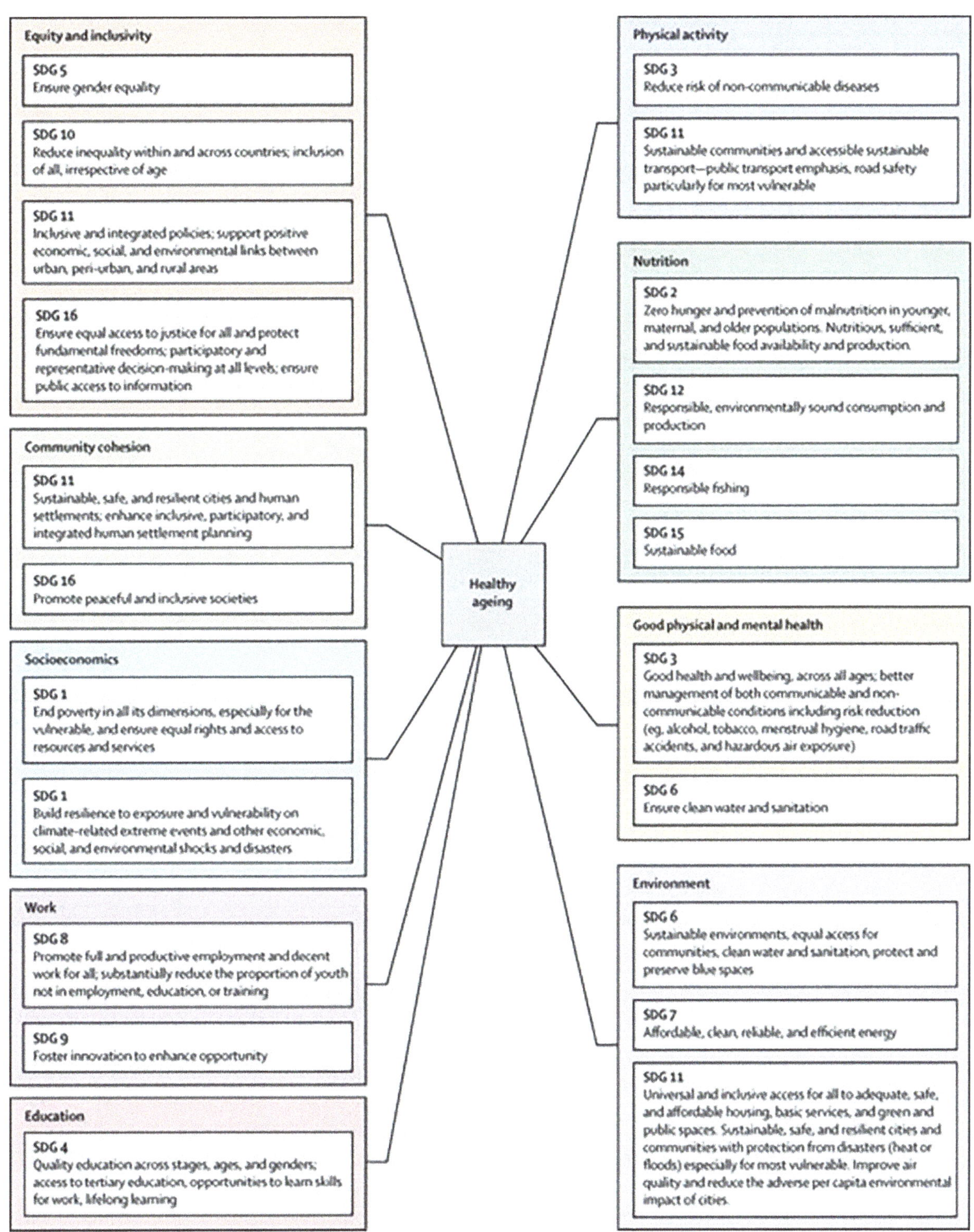

Figure 8.1: Sustainable development goals and targets mapped to factors that promote healthy aging and brain health across the lifecourse [16].

9. Enjoying Aging through Mindful Aging and Play

We all know that no one lives forever. If we take stock of what we've done, we can give consideration to opportunities the future might hold. The meaning of our lives should be told before we leave this earth and the families we leave behind.

I have written and rewritten my obituary over the last four years, each time adding to the appreciation that others have had in helping me get a sense of how to embrace life.

Brandt (2017) [20] listed several writing assignments which would help one define their value in life. For example, one exercise was to list everything you like and/or appreciate about yourself. Evaluate your ability to form the kind of friendships you want and whether you're really a person others will want to make that connection with.

There is also a compendium by Mark Evan Chimsky of things to do when you turn 80, which include: learn mindfulness, write music, walk the dog, love your relatives [23].

Through their words, we find that the aging process is not merely a period of sensory, functional, economic, and social decline. Old people continue to participate in society, and more important continue to interpret their participation in the social world. Through themes constructed from these stories, we can see how the old not only cope with losses, but how they create new meaning as they reformulate and build viable selves. Creating identity, Sharon Kaufman stresses, is a lifelong process [28]. Her " analysis (Death in hospitals) illuminates the complexity of the care of critically ill and dying patients [and] the ambiguity of slogans such as 'death with dignity,' 'quality of life,' and 'stopping life support.'… ". (From *New England Journal of Medicine* blurb on Kaufman's book).

In the Netherlands, Burzogg got started more flexible things at retirement than the traditional approach of putting them in nursing homes as they got unable to take on their own care: visiting nurses make it possible for community treatment to occur. (https://www.youtube.com/watch?v=hJCr5WJapm8).

DEATH What is your belief? ____

Despite Andrew Steele [33] telling us that Reprogramming aging can result in longer life than we have known, I believe that human beings will not live forever. We need to leave what we feel is important to tell our loved ones, our society and go with God's belief or whatever you accept as the opening of the doors to heaven after breathing stops forever.

Forget it. Look yourself in the mirror and say I am not so bad and my family loves me no matter. Stop being frail and sorry for yourself. Step up, even if you need a cane and a sometimes mobile chair and go for it. Most of all Love YOURSELF!

Laugh again. There are three books I highly recommend as a way to code what you've learned. For me Mary McHugh in her paperbacks. "How Not to Become A Little Old Lady and the companion book "How Not to Become a Crotchety Old Man " end with a smile and reminder to be who you are while you are here and don't turn off your friends and loved ones. For me the saying "Think people will be surprised when they tell them, "I'm eighty-two years old." And the crotchety old man who " Thinks it's their God-given right to drive slowly in the left lane"

In addition. we always get a heartthrob reading Dr. Seusswho writes "You're Only Old Once" [31].

Your escape plans have melted!
You haven't a chance,
for the next thing you know,
both your socks and your pants
and your drawers and your shoes
have been lost for the day
The Oglers have blossomed
Like roses in May!

Figure 9.1: The Beginning of THE END. From Dr. Seuss' *You're Only Old Once* [31].

Happiness: Lesson 82: "Happiness may seem like a young person thing," says Levitin [29]. "But the surprising thing is when older people are asked to pinpoint the happiest time of their lives, the most common response is not an age in childhood, teens, or early adulthood, it's 82."

The results are generally consistent with Paul Baltes' [1] theory of increased "wisdom" and emotional intelligence with age (at least through middle age), wherein decreased negative affective states could be a result of increasing wisdom, and with Carstensen et al.'s [5] socioemotional selectivity theory, wherein older people have an increased ability to self-regulate their emotions and view their situations positively. They are also in accord with a "positivity effect," wherein older people recall fewer negative memories than younger adults, and with the possibility that older people are more effective at regulating their emotions than younger adults. Although these theories provide a general framework for understanding increasing well-being with age, they do not predict the specific patterns of well-being shown here or the difference in Global and Hedonic well-being age profiles. A more complete understanding of the determinants of aging on well-being, including potential psychological, social, and biological explanations, deserves our attention considering the probable use of well-being as a social indicator.

10. Shifting Perspectives

Welcome to this transformative part of this final chapter of "Aging Sucks!" In this workbook-inspired chapter, we will explore the importance of aging and delve into its profound potential for personal growth, self-discovery, and embracing the beauty of life's later stages. Get ready to embark on an inspirational journey that will empower you to redefine your perspective on aging and unlock the hidden treasures that lie within.

Figure 10.1: Welcome to this transformative part of this chapter of *Aging Sucks!*

10.1 Practical Exercises

Activity 1: Reflections on Aging Take a moment to reflect on your current beliefs and attitudes towards aging. What are some negative stereotypes or societal pressures you have encountered? Write them down and challenge each one by reframing it into a positive and empowering perspective. Embrace the idea that aging is a natural and beautiful part of life, filled with wisdom, experience, and endless possibilities.

Activity 2: Gratitude for the Aging Process Create a gratitude list specifically focused on the joys and advantages that come with aging. Consider the newfound freedom, self-confidence, and opportunities that arise as we grow older. Embrace the notion that each passing year brings unique experiences and lessons that contribute to your personal growth and fulfillment.

10.2 Self-Discovery and Personal Growth

Activity 1: Exploring Life's Lessons Reflect on the valuable life lessons you have learned throughout your journey. What wisdom and insights have you gained from your experiences? Write them down and identify how they have shaped you into the person you are today. Embrace the idea that aging presents an opportunity to refine and evolve our understanding of ourselves and the world around us.

Activity 2: Setting New Goals Now is the perfect time to set new goals and aspirations for your future. Consider the dreams and passions that may have been put on hold or undiscovered during the earlier stages of life. What would you like to achieve? What steps can you take to make these goals a reality? Embrace the limitless possibilities and the newfound freedom to pursue your passions and live life to the fullest.

10.3 Cultivating Self-care and Well-being

Activity 1: Nurturing the Mind, Body, and Spirit Develop a self-care plan that encompasses physical, mental, and emotional well-being. Consider activities such as exercise, meditation, journaling, hobbies, and connecting with loved ones. Embrace the importance of self-care and prioritize your overall health and happiness as you age gracefully.

Activity 2: Embracing Change and Adaptability Change is an inevitable part of life, and as we age, it becomes increasingly important to embrace it with open arms. Reflect on past experiences where change has brought unexpected blessings or personal growth. Embrace the idea that adapting to new circumstances can lead to exciting opportunities and renewed purpose.

What are some practical exercises or activities that can help readers embrace the beauty of aging?

Here are some practical exercises and activities that can help readers embrace the beauty of aging:

1. Daily Gratitude Journal: Set aside a few minutes each day to reflect on and write down three things you are grateful for related to aging. It could be moments of joy, wisdom gained, or newfound freedom. Cultivating a gratitude practice can shift your perspective and help you appreciate the beauty in the aging process.

2. Letter to Your Younger Self: Write a heartfelt letter to your younger self, offering words of wisdom, encouragement, and reassurance. Reflect on the lessons you've learned, the challenges you've overcome, and how those experiences have shaped you into the person you are today. Embrace the growth and resilience that aging has brought you.

____

____

____

____

____

3. Self-Compassion Practice: Aging can sometimes bring self-criticism or feelings of inadequacy. Engage in self-compassion exercises, such as writing compassionate letters to yourself, practicing mindfulness, or reciting self-affirmations. Embrace self-acceptance and treat yourself with kindness and understanding as you navigate the aging process.

4. Embracing New Hobbies or Interests: Explore new hobbies or revisit old ones that bring you joy and fulfillment. It could be painting, playing a musical instrument, gardening, or learning a new language. Engaging in activities that ignite your passion can help you discover new facets of your identity and embrace the beauty of lifelong learning.

5. Connecting with Others: Foster connections with people of different age groups. Engage in intergenerational activities, volunteer in community organizations, or join clubs or groups that align with your interests. Embrace the opportunity to learn from others and share your wisdom and experiences, fostering a sense of purpose and belonging.

6. Mindful Aging Meditation: Practice mindfulness meditation specifically focused on embracing the beauty of aging. Set aside a few minutes each day to sit in a quiet space, focus on your breath, and cultivate a sense of gratitude and acceptance for the present moment. Embrace the wisdom and serenity that come with age.

7. Body Appreciation Exercises: Engage in activities that promote body appreciation and self-care. This could include gentle exercises like yoga or tai chi, taking walks in nature, engaging in mindful eating practices, or pampering yourself with self-care rituals. Embrace your body as a vessel that has carried you through life's journeys and celebrate its resilience and beauty.

8. Lifelong Learning: Engage in intellectual pursuits and lifelong learning. Attend lectures, enroll in online courses, join book clubs, or explore topics of interest through reading or documentaries. Embrace the opportunity to expand your knowledge and stimulate your mind, reinforcing the idea that aging is a continuous process of growth and intellectual development.

____

____

____

____

____

Remember, embracing the beauty of aging is a personal and individual journey. Choose activities that resonate with you and align with your interests, values, and aspirations. Embrace the process with an open heart and a willingness to explore new horizons as you navigate the wonderful stages of life.

10.4 Conclusion

Congratulations on completing this transformative book! You have embarked on a journey of self-discovery and redefined your perspective on aging. Remember, aging is not the end of a vibrant life; it is the beginning of a new chapter filled with endless possibilities, wisdom, and personal growth. Embrace the beauty of aging and live each day with purpose, gratitude, and an unwavering belief in your own strength and resilience.

Figure 10.2: Oprah on Aging: "To me, aging well means feeling fit and strong—emotionally and physically—and being fully self-aware to the point of self-actualization."

The World is Breaking in Flowers the Breath of Things
By: Precious Okayamon

Our love is a blue instant and forward-looking sky
Every dream is a moment of freedom

Bliss hovering above the void

Resonate darkness can't be bound
It's always being born

Ash in hand

Myths arise where it sets
Knowing there is fire
Knowing there is war

Cities rising and falling

A small black river flowing
The speed of darkness
Everything burns repeatedly

Return back to the umbilical tongue
To vesicles of present breath

Swallow bits of tenderness
Bring yourself back to the earth

Bibliography

Articles

[1] Paul B Baltes. "Extending longevity: Dignity gain-or dignity drain?" In: *MaxPlanckResearch* 3 (2003), pages 15–19 (cited on page 45).

[2] Jamila Bookwala and Trent Gaugler. "Relationship quality and 5-year mortality risk." In: *Health Psychology* 39.8 (2020), pages 633–641 (cited on page 6).

[3] Lisa Bowleg. "The problem with the phrase women and minorities: intersectionality—an important theoretical framework for public health". In: *American journal of public health* 102.7 (2012), pages 1267–1273 (cited on page 40).

[4] Gail F Brenner, Barbara G Melamed, and Richard S Panush. "Optimism and coping as determinants of psychosocial adjustment to rheumatoid arthritis". In: *Journal of Clinical Psychology in Medical Settings* 1 (1994), pages 115–134 (cited on page 40).

[5] Laura L Carstensen, Helene H Fung, and Susan T Charles. "Socioemotional selectivity theory and the regulation of emotion in the second half of life". In: *Motivation and emotion* 27 (2003), pages 103–123 (cited on page 45).

[6] Miranda Corpora. "The Privilege of a Good Death: An Intersectional Perspective on Dy- ing a Good Death in America". In: *The Gerontologist* 62.5 (2021), pages 773–779. ISSN: 0016-9013. DOI: 10. 1093/ geront/ gnab130. eprint: https:// academic. oup. com/ gerontologist / article - pdf / 62... 773 / 43858013 / gnab130 . pdf. URL: https://doi.org/10.1093/geront/gnab130 (cited on page 40).

[7] Timothy A Donlon et al. "FOXO3, a resilience gene: Impact on lifespan, healthspan, and deathspan". In: *The Journals of Gerontology: Series A* 77.8 (2022), pages 1479–1484 (cited on page 37).

[8] James D Doorley et al. "Feasibility randomized controlled trial of a mind–body activity program for older adults with chronic pain and cognitive decline: the virtual "Active Brains" study". In: *The Gerontologist* 62.7 (2022), pages 1082–1094 (cited on page 38).

[9] Karen L Fingerman et al. "Television viewing, physical activity, and loneliness in late life". In: *The Gerontologist* 62.7 (2022), pages 1006–1017 (cited on page 29).

[10] Jessica A Hehman and Daphne Blunt Bugental. "Responses to patronizing communication and factors that attenuate those responses." In: *Psychology and Aging* 30.3 (2015), page 552 (cited on page 41).

[11] Thomas Nicolaj Iversen, Lars Larsen, and Per Erik Solem. "A conceptual analysis of ageism". In: *Nordic psychology* 61.3 (2009), pages 4–22 (cited on page 33).

[12] John S Ji et al. "Effect of FOXO3 and air pollution on cognitive function: a longitudinal cohort study of older adults in China from 2000 to 2014". In: *The Journals of Gerontology: Series A* 77.8 (2022), pages 1534–1541 (cited on page 37).

[13] Becca R Levy, Mahazarin R Banaji, and Todd Nelson. "Ageism: Stereotyping and prejudice against older persons". In: *Implicit ageism* (2002), pages 49–7 (cited on page 34).

[14] Becca R Levy et al. "Association between positive age stereotypes and recovery from disability in older persons". In: *Jama* 308.19 (2012), pages 1972–1973 (cited on page 34).

[15] Hara Estroff Marano. "The Best Diet to Maintain Your Brain". In: *Psychology Today* (May 2023). URL: https://www.psychologytoday.com/us/articles/202305/the-best- diet-to-maintain-your-brain (cited on page 29).

[16] Angelique Mavrodaris, Louise Lafortune, and Carol E Brayne. "The future longevity: designing a synergistic approach for healthy ageing, sustainability, and equity". In: *The Lancet Healthy Longevity* 3.9 (2022), e584–e586. DOI: 10.1016/S2666-7568(22)00145-3. URL: https://doi.org/10.1016/S2666-7568(22)00145-3 (cited on page 42).

[17] Wee Kheng Soo et al. "Integrated Geriatric Assessment and Treatment Effectiveness (INTE-GERATE) in older people with cancer starting systemic anticancer treatment in Australia: a multicentre, open-label, randomised controlled trial". In: *The Lancet Healthy Longevity* 3.9 (2024/09/29 2022), e617–e627. DOI: 10.1016/S2666-7568(22)00169-6 (cited on page 37).

[18] Staff. "Oral health in America: A report of the Surgeon General". In: *U.S. Department of Health and Human Services* (2000). URL: https… www . nidcr . nih . gov / sites / default / files / 2017 - 10 / hck1ocv . %40www . surgeon . fullrpt . pdf (cited on page 20).

[19] Staff. "Living Longer and Better". In: *National Geographic* (Jan. 2023) (cited on page 5).

Books

[20.] A. Brandt. *Mindful Aging: Embracing Your Life After 50 to Find Fulfillment, Purpose, and Joy.* PESI Publishing & Media, 2017. ISBN: 9781683730781. URL: https://books. google.com/books?id=EA_wswEACAAJ (cited on page 43).

[21.] D. Bredesen. *The End of Alzheimer's: The First Program to Prevent and Reverse Cognitive Decline.* New York: Penguin Publishing Group, 2017. ISBN: 9780735216204. URL: https://books. google.com/books?id=YtwtDwAAQBAJ (cited on page 28).

[22.] J. Carper. *Stop Aging Now!: The Ultimate Plan for Staying Young and Reversing the Aging Process.* HarperCollins, 1995. ISBN: 9780060183554. URL: https://books.google.com/books?id=XJduPwAACAAJ (cited on pages 4, 5).

[23.] M.E. Chimsky. *80 Things to Do When You Turn 80: 80 Experts on the Subject of Turning 80.* Sellers Publishing, Incorporated, 2017. ISBN: 9781416246107. URL: https://books. google.com/books?id=ZoohvgAACAAJ (cited on page 43).

[24.] David ZJ Chu. *Prevent Cancer and Fix What Aging Ails You.* BookBaby, 2020 (cited on page 41).

[25.] Eric Erikson. *Childhood and Society.* New York: W. W. Norton Press, 1950 (cited on page 35).

[26.] A. Huffington. *Thrive: The Third Metric to Redefining Success and Creating a Life of Well-Being, Wisdom, and Wonder.* Harmony/Rodale, 2014. ISBN: 9780804140850. URL: https://books.google. com/books?id=MIUpAgAAQBAJ (cited on page 4).

[27.] J.A. Jenkins. *Disrupt Aging: A Bold New Path to Living Your Best Life at Every Age.* PublicAffairs, 2016. ISBN: 9781610396769. URL: https://books.google.com/books? id=OfLQDQAAQBAJ (cited on page 4).

[28.] S.R. Kaufman. *The Ageless Self: Sources of Meaning in Late Life*. A Meridian book. New American Library, 1987. ISBN: 9780452008885. URL: https://books.google.com/books?id=WR9FAAAAYAAJ (cited on page 43).

[29.] D.J. Levitin. *Successful Aging: A Neuroscientist Explores the Power and Potential of Our Lives*. Penguin Publishing Group, 2020. ISBN: 9781524744199. URL: https://books. google.com/books?id=7yeZDwAAQBAJ (cited on page 44).

[30.] A.J. Marsella and G. White. *Cultural Conceptions of Mental Health and Therapy*. Culture, Illness and Healing. Netherlands: Springer, 1982. ISBN: 9789027713629. URL: https ://books.google.com/books?id=P6Xpf87G1W4C (cited on page 21).

[31.] Dr. Seuss. *You're Only Old Once!: A Book for Obsolete Children*. New York: Random House Children's Books, 1986. ISBN: 9780385379502. URL: https:// books. google. com/books?id=3LHxAwAAQBAJ (cited on page 44).

[32.] D.A. Sinclair and M.D. LaPlante. *Lifespan: Why We Age—and Why We Don't Have To*. Atria Books, 2019. ISBN: 9781501191978. URL: https://books.google.com/books?id=x-- oDwAAQBAJ (cited on page 5).

[33.] A. Steele. *Ageless: The New Science of Getting Older Without Getting Old*. Knopf Doubleday Publishing Group, 2021. ISBN: 9780385544931. URL: https://books.google.com/books?id=Z2esDwAAQBAJ (cited on pages 4, 43).

[34.] G. Vaillant. *Aging Well*. New York: Little, Brown Spark Hachette Book Group, 2002 (cited on page 34).

[35.] H. Wang and C.U. Grosse. *Chinese for Business and Professionals in the Workplace: Reach- ing Across Disciplines*. London: Routledge, 2022. ISBN: 9780367857349. URL: https ://books.google. com/books?id=ibPozgEACAAJ (cited on page 22).

Online

[36.] Liat Ayalon and Clemens Tesch-Römer. *Taking a closer look at ageism: Self-and other- directed ageist attitudes and discrimination*. 2017 (cited on page 33).

[37.] Sonya Collins. *Is There a Cure for Aging? Why some researchers are hopeful about human immortality*. https://www.webmd.com/healthy- aging/story/is- there- a- cure- for-aging. Feb. 2021 (cited on page 27).

[38.] Patrick J. Kiger and Rachel Nania. *10 Early Warning Signs of Dementia You Shouldn't Ignore*. https :// www . aarp . org / caregiving / health / info - 2019 / dementia - warning - signs.html. July 2024 (cited on page 27).

[39.] Mia McNiece. *Jane Fonda on Why at 85 She's the Happiest She's Ever Been: 'Life Gets Better with Age' (Exclusive)*. People Magazine https://people.com/movies/jane- fonda- why-happiest-shes-ever-been-life-gets-better-with-age-exclusive/. May 2023 (cited on page 34).

[40.] *National Center for Complementary and Integrative Health*. Sept. 2024. URL: https ://www.nccih. nih.gov/ (cited on page 6).

[41.] *National Social Life, Health & Aging Project*. 2024. URL: https :// www . norc . org / research/ projects/national- social- life- health- and- aging- project.html (cited on page 6).

[42.] Paula Span. *A Great Credit Score, but She Can't Get a Mortgage*. https://www.nytimes. com/2023/04/08/health/mortgage-loan-credit-score-financials.html. Apr. 8 (cited on page 34).